MW01122450

ABOUT MAGIC READERS

ABDO continues its commitment to quality books with the nonfiction Magic Readers series. This series includes three levels of books to help students progress to being independent readers while learning factual information. Different levels are intended to reflect the stages of reading in the early grades, helping to select the best level for each individual student.

Level 1: Books with short sentences and familiar words or patterns to share with children who are beginning to understand how letters and sounds go together.

Level 2: Books with longer words and sentences and more complex language patterns with less repetition for progressing readers who are practicing common words and letter sounds.

Level 3: Books with more developed language and vocabulary for transitional readers who are using strategies to figure out unknown words and are ready to learn information more independently.

These nonfiction readers are aligned with the Common Core State Standards progression of literacy, following the sequence of skills and increasing the difficulty of language while engaging the curious minds of young children. These books also reflect the increasing importance of reading informational material in the early grades. They encourage children to read for fun and to learn!

Hannah E. Tolles, MA Reading Specialist

www.abdopublishing.com

Published by Magic Wagon, a division of ABDO, PO Box 398166, Minneapolis, Minnesota 55439. Copyright © 2015 by Abdo Consulting Group, Inc. International copyrights reserved in all countries. No part of this book may be reproduced in any form without written permission from the publisher. Magic Readers™ is a trademark and logo of Magic Wagon.

Printed in the United States of America, North Mankato, Minnesota.
062014
092014

THIS BOOK CONTAINS
RECYCLED MATERIALS

Cover Photo: Thinkstock
Interior Photos: iStockphoto, Shutterstock, Thinkstock

Written and edited by Rochelle Baltzer, Heidi M. D. Elston,
  Megan M. Gunderson, and Bridget O'Brien
Illustrated by Candice Keimig
Designed by Candice Keimig and Jillian O'Brien

Library of Congress Cataloging-in-Publication Data

O'Brien, Bridget, 1991- author.
  Deer eat and grow / written and edited by Bridget O'Brien [and three others] ;
designed and illustrated by Candice Keimig.
     pages cm. -- (Magic readers. Level 2)
  Audience: Ages 5-8.
  ISBN 978-1-62402-064-3
  1. White-tailed deer--Juvenile literature. 2. Fawns--Juvenile literature. I. Keimig,
Candice, illustrator. II. Title.
  QL737.U55O272 2015
  599.65'2--dc23
                    2014005840

Magic Readers

level
2

Deer
Eat and Grow

By Bridget O'Brien
Illustrated photos by Candice Keimig

Magic Readers

An Imprint of Magic Wagon
www.abdopublishing.com

This is a baby white-tailed deer.

It is called a fawn.

Deer often have twins.

Fawns can walk right away!

A fawn is reddish-brown with white spots.

A fawn loses its spots by its first winter.

A fawn lives with its mother.

It drinks her milk for a few weeks.

A mother deer keeps her fawns safe.

When she goes away to eat,

the fawns hide.

Deer eat in early morning and late afternoon.

They eat buds, twigs, and
nuts.

Deer drink water.

Sometimes in winter, they eat snow.

A full-grown male deer is called a buck.

A female is called a doe.

A buck grows antlers.

It sheds them each year.

Deer can grow to more than 200 pounds.

They can be 4 feet tall.

Most deer live 2 to 3 years.

Some live more than 20!